IT'S TIME TO EAT SAUERKRAUT

It's Time to Eat SAUERKRAUT

Walter the Educator

Silent King Books
A WhichHead Entertainment Imprint

Copyright © 2024 by Walter the Educator

All rights reserved. No part of this book may be reproduced in any manner whatsoever without written per- mission except in the case of brief quotations embodied in critical articles and reviews.

First Printing, 2024

Disclaimer

This book is a literary work; the story is not about specific persons, locations, situations, and/or circumstances unless mentioned in a historical context. Any resemblance to real persons, locations, situations, and/or circumstances is coincidental. This book is for entertainment and informational purposes only. The author and publisher offer this information without warranties expressed or implied. No matter the grounds, neither the author nor the publisher will be accountable for any losses, injuries, or other damages caused by the reader's use of this book. The use of this book acknowledges an understanding and acceptance of this disclaimer.

It's Time to Eat SAUERKRAUT is a collectible early learning book by Walter the Educator suitable for all ages belonging to Walter the Educator's Time to Eat Book Series. Collect more books at WaltertheEducator.com

USE THE EXTRA SPACE TO TAKE NOTES AND DOCUMENT YOUR MEMORIES

SAUERKRAUT

It's time to eat sauerkraut today,

It's Time to Eat
Sauerkraut

A tangy treat in a special way.

It's made from cabbage, thin and neat,

Fermented fun that's hard to beat!

With every bite, it's sour and bright,

A crunchy snack that feels just right.

You might say, "Oh, it's not so sweet,"

But sauerkraut's a tasty feat!

On hot dogs, sandwiches, or just alone,

This cabbage dish has made its home.

It's tangy, zippy, full of zing,

A bite of joy that makes you sing!

Sauerkraut's good for your tummy, too,

Helping you feel happy and new.

It's full of crunch, a little surprise,

A snack that's healthy and so wise!

It's Time to Eat
Sauerkraut

Do you like it plain or with a spice?

Add a forkful, it's really nice!

You might say, "What's this all about?"

But soon you'll love your sauerkraut!

Its sour taste is quite a treat,

A little tang, and you'll say, "Neat!"

It starts as cabbage, fresh and green,

Then turns into a food machine!

From Germany to lands afar,

Sauerkraut's a food superstar!

People love it far and wide,

A sour crunch in every bite.

Let's grab a bowl, let's scoop it out,

It's time to eat that sauerkraut!

Don't be shy, give it a try,

It's Time to Eat
Sauerkraut

It's healthy food, you'll soon know why!

So munch and crunch, let's all agree,

Sauerkraut is the snack for me!

It's time to eat, so dig right in,

A tangy treat that makes you grin!

Now every time you hear its name,

You'll think of sauerkraut's tasty fame.

A sour snack that's fun to chew,

It's Time to Eat
Sauerkraut

It's time to eat, just right for you!

ABOUT THE CREATOR

Walter the Educator is one of the pseudonyms for Walter Anderson. Formally educated in Chemistry, Business, and Education, he is an educator, an author, a diverse entrepreneur, and he is the son of a disabled war veteran. "Walter the Educator" shares his time between educating and creating. He holds interests and owns several creative projects that entertain, enlighten, enhance, and educate, hoping to inspire and motivate you. Follow, find new works, and stay up to date with Walter the Educator™

at WaltertheEducator.com

www.ingramcontent.com/pod-product-compliance
Lightning Source LLC
LaVergne TN
LVHW010411070526
838199LV00064B/5260